Moral Compass
Pro

Anthony H. Normore, Ph.D.

Mitch Javidi, Ph.D.

Terry Anderson, Ph.D.

Sheriff Newell Normand

Lt. Col. Wellington R. Scott, Sr., Ret.

Lt. Christopher Hoina, Ret.

Printed in the United of States of America
First Edition: March 2014
Library of Congress Cataloging-in-Publication Data
International Academy of Public Safety, Inc.

Moral Compass For Law Enforcement Professionals

ISBN - 978-1-4951-0818-1

Printed in the United States of America
1 2 3 4 5 6 7 8 9 10

This book is dedicated to all men and women of Law Enforcement who are accountable for Peace, are sentinels of Justice, and are committed to Service and Equity!

"Every Officer is a Leader"

Ria -

We have, we are and always will live our lives with a Moral Compass. Your Brother in Cause -

Mitch

"Human progress is neither automatic nor inevitable... Every step toward the goal of justice requires sacrifice, suffering, and struggle; the tireless exertions and passionate concern of dedicated individuals."

Martin Luther King, Jr.

"There is but one law for all, namely that law which governs all law, the law of our Creator, the law of humanity, justice, equity - the law of nature and of nations."

Edmund Burke

Advanced Praise for the Book

"Moral Compass for Law Enforcement Professionals dives into the concepts of what separates good leaders from great ones; character. *It addresses the key principles of great leadership, encourages role modeling and self-reflection through reassuring the enabling of values described within. This handbook is a great guide for those men and women in law enforcement who desire successful personal and professional development."*

Dr. Timothy W. Turner, *Ed.D., MSCJ,* Professor, Anderson and Columbia Southern Universities, FBI (Ret.)

"This unique resource is essential for law enforcement officers and other public safety personnel. The authors have condensed into a highly concentrated book the essentials that leaders need to become aware of the core of their ethical commitments."

Ward Clapham
Superintendent, Royal Canadian Mounted Police (Ret.)

"Law enforcement has always depended on trusting relationships among officers, leaders, agencies, and the public. The authors ably describe, a police leader must earn trust through a moral and ethical commitment. Effective policing requires that your colleagues know that you will maintain the highest standards of conduct in all situations, regardless of difficulties or consequences. I recommend their work to every police leader, in other words to every police professional."

Dr. John Morgan, Former Director of the Office of Science and Technology in the DOJ National Institute of Justice

"The supreme quality for leadership is unquestionably integrity. Without it, no real success is possible, no matter whether it is on a section gang, a football field, in an army, or in an office."

Dwight D. Eisenhower

"Tragedy in life normally comes with betrayal and compromise, and trading on your integrity and not having dignity in life. That's really where failure comes."

Tom Cochrane

Forward

"Leadership is a potent combination of strategy and character. But if you must be without one, be without the strategy."

– General Norman Schwarzkopf

General Schwarzkopf recognized the vital role that character plays in the life of a leader. Competencies (knowledge, skills, abilities, tactics, planning, strategic thinking, etc.) are important also. But out of the two, character is the MOST important. Think about it this way: up to this point in your career, how much of your training has been competency-based versus how much has been character-based? When I ask that question to law enforcement leaders around the globe, I invariably get an answer that somewhere between 80-100% has been competency-based--training that focuses on expanding a knowledge base or enhancing a skill set. Yet, on which side of this equation are almost ALL of our problems?

I mean, when is the last time someone in your organization was terminated for a lack of competency? They couldn't qualify on the firing range. They couldn't pass the emergency vehicle operation course. They couldn't fill out a report properly. They couldn't process a crime scene or testify in court effectively. Sure, it happens. But when was the last time THAT happened as opposed to someone was terminated for lying to a supervisor? For taking something that didn't belong to them? For falsifying a police report? For embezzling money out of the jail commissary fund? For abusing a handcuffed prisoner? Or for taking indecent liberties with an informant or an inmate? These are the types of issues that are killing us in our profession. While most of our training centers on skill-building, most of our problems stem from ethical failures.

That's where the International Academy of Public Safety team comes in. Led by Drs. Anthony Normore (Tony) and Mitch Javidi (President of IAPS), *Moral Compass for Law Enforcement Professionals* is a timely and significant contribution to the arena of public safety. Our training seeks to enhance both competency AND character, with a heavy emphasis on the latter. Dr. Anderson is right when he asserts that, "Every officer is a leader." I couldn't agree more. As caretakers of the "law, order, health, safety, and morals" of a community, each officer is, and by rights ought to be, held to the highest of standards in all five of these arenas.

This book is a fantastic primer on the principles of character, leadership, and professional ethics that will provide clear direction for your journey through the often confusing challenges that are sure to present themselves during your career as a public safety officer. Our hopes are that, by understanding and internalizing these foundational principles, you will be empowered to successfully navigate the "path of most resistance," the path of leadership.

Sheriff Ray Nash, Ret.
President - Police Dynamics Institute, Inc.
Sr. Vice-President of Training and Development - International Academy of Public Safety

Acknowledgements

"Whom shall I send? And who will go for us?" And I said,
"Here am I. Send me!"

Isaiah 6:8

We would like to express our gratitude to the many people who inspired us to write this book; who reinforced the spirit of this body of work; who exemplified its nature by their good deeds and their dedication to the ideals of peace, equity, service and justice.

We thank the team at IAPS. We realize over the years of development we have been lucky enough to interact with great people that kept us on course. We especially thank Mr. Dwight Paulsen for his focus on good character, leadership, and continued support; without him the realization of IAPS and this book would not be possible.

We must recognize the Jefferson Parish Sheriff's Office and their progressive men and women who allowed us into their lives, to ask difficult questions, and act as a focus group so other law enforcement practitioners could benefit. Special thanks go to Major Kerry Najolia, Chief Steve Lachute and Attorney Timmy Valenti for their vision and contributions to our thinking. Deep gratitude goes to Chief Alan Smith and Sara O'Brien of the Atlantic Beach Police Department for the editorial support and contributions to our thinking. Special Thanks goes to Dorian Javidi (US Air Force Officer Training School), Alexander Javidi (IAPS' Field Command Articulation Manager), and Lorraine Snyder (NC Department of Crime Control and Public Safety and Law Enforcement Instructor) for their creative leadership thinking.

Our greatest esteem and admiration are extended to the incomparable visionary and accomplished leaders who serve as our mentors: General Hugh Shelton, General William Boykin, General Colin Powel, Colonel Craig Kozeniesky, Attorney General Van Hollen, Administrator Brian O'Keefe, Attorney General Marty Jackley, Secretary James LeBlanc, Under-Secretary Thomas Bickham, Pam Laborde, Secretary Frank Perry, Colonel William Grey, Colonel Craig Price, Colonel Michael Edmonson, Colonel Michael Gilchrist (NC DPS Ret.), Colonel Allen Witt, Major Tory Butler, Major Mark Sawa, Executive Director Michael Ranatza, Director Bryan Gortmaker, Director Dan Satterlee, Director Tony Barthuly, Director Mark Strickland, Sheriff B.J. Barnes, Sheriff Asa Buck, Sheriff Richard Webster, Sheriff Greg Champagne, Sheriff Van Duncan, Sheriff Adrian Garcia, Sheriff Lonnie Greco, Sheriff Greg Hamilton, Sheriff Daniel Edwards, Sheriff Jason Ard, Chief Joseph Cardella, Chief Jack Lewis (Apex NC Police Ret.), Sheriff Michael Leidholt, Sheriff Dean Meyer, Sheriff David Mahoney, Sheriff Mike Milstead, Sheriff Susan Pamerleau (Ret. USAF General), Chief Mike Dickey, Sheriff Robert Spoden, Commander Troy Knudson, Sheriff Tony Perry, Chief Mark Perez of LAPD, Sheriff Kevin Thom, Sheriff Mike Tregre, Sheriff Jeff Wiley, Captain Dan Bolch, and Captain Ruggles.

Special thanks also goes to our select Subject Matter Experts (SMEs), strategic partners, and instructors who lead us with their Law Enforcement expertise and principles on ethical leadership everyday: Sherry Bass, Dr. Tim Turner, Dr. Neal Trautman, Dr. Larry Long, Lt. Colonel Levin (US National Guards Ret.), Lt. Colonel Ted Spain (US Army Ret.), Master Sergeant Paul Howe (USASOC, Ret.), Commander Charles "Sid" Heal, Lt. Col. Tim

Anderson (US Marines Ret.), Commander Odie Odenthal, Chief Gary Benthin, Chief Deputy Gary Blankenship (Ret.), Chief Deputy Ben Bailey, Sheriff Ray Nash, Capt. Tracy Kelly, Chief Percy Crutchfield, and Deputy Chief Mike Robinson.

We give gratitude to the institutions and agencies that have encouraged and inspired us to grow as leaders. They include but are not limited to the Universities and Academies we attended, the International Association of Chiefs of Police, The National Sheriff's Association, the International Association of Directors of Law Enforcement Standards and Training (IADLEST), Military Police Corps, Army National Guard, National Institute of Ethics, US Army, US Air Force, FBI National Academy, FBI LEEDA, West Point, IACP's LPO, Southern Police Institute Leadership, and the Northwestern leadership program. We would like to acknowledge our friends and families, who have supported us individually to do our best, make a contribution to our communities and make a difference. Our families give us the strength to be the people we have become. We thank them for allowing us to spend so much time away from them and hope they understand.

Finally, to all public safety personnel, and others whose names we may have inadvertently failed to mention; you offered comments, ideas, rewrites, proofreading, edits, design input and remarks to help shape our ideas; we truly appreciate all you have contributed. Without you, this book would not have been made possible.

Normore, et. al.

"I refuse to accept the view that mankind is so tragically bound to the starless midnight of racism and war that the bright daybreak of peace and brotherhood can never become a reality... I believe that unarmed truth and unconditional love will have the final word."

Martin Luther King, Jr.

"You will reciprocally promise love, loyalty and matrimonial honesty. We only want for you this day that these words constitute the principle of your entire life and that with the help of divine grace you will observe these solemn vows that today, before God, you formulate."

Pope John Paul II

Introduction

The executive team at the International Academy of Public Safety (IAPS) is proud to introduce this practical resource book designed specifically for the field of law enforcement. Replete with personal and professional experiences, proven best practices, and supported by evidence-based research, our book is not intended to be a how-to manual with step-by-step instructions – the lives of those in law enforcement rarely follow a blueprint. Rather, it is styled as a "go-to" moral compass intended to guide the overall thinking for those whose daily duties include serving and protecting the public.

> *"Treat those who are good with goodness, and also treat those who are not good with goodness. Thus goodness is attained. Be honest to those who are honest, and be also honest to those who are not honest. Thus honesty is attained."*
>
> *Tao Tzu*

Our mission at IAPS is multi-purposed: to provide training that enhances the professionalism, accountability, leadership, and readiness of law enforcement agencies; and to foster values-based credible leadership, ethical practices, positive attitudes, moral literacy/fortitude and responsibility, principled behaviors among law enforcement professionals. The tools that we provide enrich and reinforce these characteristics in a manner easily delivered to all professionals who work in the public safety sector. This guide however, is specifically adapted to address those in the law enforcement division of this arena.

It is our belief that that "every officer is a leader" (Anderson, Gisborne, & Holliday, 2012) and as such is expected to be a model of positive influence within the scope of his/her responsibility. We hope that referencing this guide will assist officers in ensuring that their actions reflect their police agency's mission, vision, philosophy, values, and school of thought.

After much team reflection it seemed appropriate to introduce this book metaphorically as a "compass". By "compass" we mean a simple instrument that, with its northward facing needle, is a consistent and correct indicator of direction. By adding the word "moral" we hope to evoke a clear picture of those values that will always steer an officer in a virtuous direction. Some may argue that morals are situationally dependent, but *as law enforcement officers our "moral compass" should always point in the same direction, no matter which way we turn, no matter who is (or is not) watching.*

Purpose and Organization of the Book

This book is intended to serve as a moral compass for you as you navigate the challenges and demands that confront you as police officers. Among these challenges and demands are the operational crime control and the order maintenance functions of police in society (e.g., drug-trafficking, violent crime, public disorder, gangs, active shooter, etc.).

Our purpose is to encourage you to always respond in ways that are consistent not only with society's expectations, but also with the law. You are responsible and accountable to the political environment, yet you must not allow yourself to be vulnerable to inappropriate political interference or control (e.g., police operations, criminal investigations).

We introduce *Moral Compass for Law Enforcement Professionals* by first providing a general understanding of the key concepts. Next, we present a brief overview of the key concepts that we consider to be pivotal in the formation of character development for law enforcement leadership. This is followed by a description of the cornerstones upon which the foundation of our academy rests.

> *"A tree is known by its fruit; a man by his deeds. A good deed is never lost; he who sows courtesy reaps friendship, and he who plants kindness gathers love."*
>
> *Saint Basil*

Then, we introduce "moral courage" and "personal and professional codes of ethics" to help contextualize the heart of the book - we also include a series of credible leadership values in tabular format intended to be routinely used by you and members of your agency. Next, we offer a few final reflections and concluding remarks. The book then closes with a short reference list.

As you use this guide, keep in mind that people "listen" with their eyes as well as with their ears. Character is judged not only by the words that you say, but also by the actions that you take. *Consistent role modeling coupled with ongoing self-reflection and education in ethics, values, and virtues, is an authentic combination for personal and professional success.*

Key Concept: Ethics

Ethics has a long and varied history. Researchers agree the concept stems from Greek and Roman Philosophy and involved discourse around Hedonism, Epicurus, Cynics, Stoicism, and Skeptics. Among the litany of philosophers who studied ethics over time are Aristotle and Marcus Aurelius Antoninus (from the Classical Period). From the Modern Period we were introduced to the likes of Immanuel Kant, Thomas Hobbes, Jeremy Bentham and Jean-Jacques Rousseau. In the Contemporary Period we have come to know the works of Simone de Beauvoir, John Dewey, Michel Foucault, Carl Jung, Jurgen Habermas, Lawrence Kohlberg, Edith Stein, Viktor Frankl, and Jean-Paul Sartre – to name a few. According to Resnik (2011), people tend to think of ethics as "rules for distinguishing between right and wrong, such as the Golden Rule ("Do unto others as you would have them do unto you"), a code of professional conduct like the Hippocratic Oath ("First of all, do no harm"), a religious creed like the Ten Commandments ("Thou Shalt not kill..."), or wise aphorisms like the sayings of Confucius... that distinguish between acceptable and unacceptable behavior" (para.1).

It's hard to imagine how humans handled difficult situations before the advent of writing. Surely, they wrestled with ethical issues, and must have confronted challenging situations that required reflection about the right way to act. You will not get an argument from us that ethics is a complex issue. Perhaps you might ask "why?" We believe, as others do, it is because the subject matter is human conduct. Conduct does not merely occur but emanates from the totality of the person. Conduct implies that we have a choice (Resnik, 2011).

We intentionally choose one course of action over another with the understanding that our conduct is rational. Rebore (2014) shares the classical beginnings of ethical considerations when he takes us back to Plato's account of Socrate's trial and his search for truth.

Socrates was accused of disturbing the social order "because he went through Athens asking citizens their opinions concerning the ultimate meaning of human existence. At his trial, he accepted the death penalty and drank hemlock rather than give up his search for truth" (p. 5). For Socrates, the unexamined life is not worth living. According to John Dewey (1916), ethics is the science that deals with conduct insofar as this is considered to be right or wrong, good or bad. Ethics comes from the Greek word *ethos* which means "customs or usages, especially belonging to one group as distinguished from another" (Shapiro & Stefkovich, 2011, p. 11). Later, ethics came to mean disposition of character, customs, and approved ways of acting.

For our purposes, the ultimate goal of ethics is to establish standards of conduct, a disciplined way of thinking, and to provide a unique kind of response to issues in law enforcement and law enforcement leadership. They are standards or codes of behavior expected by the group to which the individual belongs; a social system in which morals are applied (e.g., family ethics, professional ethics, social ethics, organizational/agency ethics, national ethics).

Key Concepts: Morals

Morals define personal character; they are values which we "attribute to a system of beliefs, typically a spiritual or religious system, but it could also be attributed to a political system or some other set of beliefs" (Navran, 2014, para.2). In society today political correctness, rules and people find themselves avoiding framing ethical choices in moral terms for fear that doing so might prove offensive to some.

> *"About morals, I know only that what is moral is what you feel good after and what is immoral is what you feel bad after."*
>
> *Ernest Hemingway*

Many individuals' values are strongly influenced by a sense of morality –right as defined by a higher authority. Yet they refrain from citing that authority "because doing so may seem less rational and more emotional to others who do not share the same belief system" (para. 3). The lack of public reference however; to morals, does not diminish the power of moral authority.

Key Concepts: Ethics vs. Morals

Differentiating between ethics and morals can be difficult. They both deal with the concept of right and wrong, but ethics are external standards, whereas morals are personal principles. Ethics are provided by the institutions, groups or culture to which an individual belongs (e.g., a police agency).

For example, police officers all have to follow an ethical code laid down by the law enforcement profession, regardless of their own feelings or preferences. Ethics are considered part of a social system or a framework for acceptable behavior (Taylor, 1991).

> *"A man without ethics is a wild beast loosed upon this world."*
>
> *Albert Camus*

Morals may also be influenced by culture or society, but they are personal principles created and upheld by the individuals themselves (Starratt, 2004).

Let us consider a criminal defense lawyer. Though the lawyer's personal moral code finds murder immoral and reprehensible, ethics demand the accused client be defended as vigorously as possible, even when the lawyer knows the party is guilty and that a freed defendant would potentially lead to more crime.

In this case, legal ethics override personal morals for the greater good of upholding a justice system in which the accused is given a fair trial and the prosecution must prove guilt beyond a reasonable doubt (Anderson, Gisborne, & Holliday, 2012).

Key Concepts: Values

Values are our fundamental beliefs. According to Navran (2014), they are the principles we use to define that which is right, good and just. They provide guidance as we determine The Right versus The Wrong, The Good versus The Bad. They are our standards, and refer to all important beliefs. They are "personal preferences" meaning they are personal choices that are subjective and changeable anytime (e.g., car, house). They are also "principles", meaning they are consistent, transcultural and objective (e.g., honesty, fairness).

Not all values are ethical, some are neutral or even non-ethical; what we say versus what we do (Navran, 2014). When trying to set priorities in life, it is very important to have a firm grasp on the values that are important to you.

> *"Through mutual understanding, sincerity and goodwill, and with great wisdom and broad views, the leaders on both sides should jointly initiate new opportunities for peace, stability, cooperation and mutual benefit."*
>
> *Chen Shui-Bian*

Normally, the values that have shaped your life are part of your personality and generally go hand-in-hand with your character.

Key Concepts: Virtues

Virtues are positive traits or qualities deemed to be morally good; when we define virtue, we deem it as objective, an actual quality considered morally good or desirable in a person. As Aristotle suggested, virtue is a state of excellence along a continuum from deficit to excess (Aristotle, 2003). Aristotle noted this balance as the Golden Mean; Confucius wrote similarly about the Doctrine of the Mean (Legge, 1893).

> *"Our virtues and our failings are inseparable, like force and matter. When they separate, man is no more."*
>
> *Nikola Tesla*

As one's principles are grounded in virtue, leadership through care-based reciprocity is achievable. It is important to note however that Aristotle separated moral from intellectual virtues. He described "intellectual" as wisdom (generally from teaching...) and "moral" as feeling, choosing and then acting (well) along the continuum between excess and deficiency.

His, and Plato's, belief was that the pursuit of eudemonia (e.g., happiness or good spirit) was the ultimate goal to live a happy life, and also necessary for the perfect polis (the city to which Socrates was dedicated). Aristotle, and later St. Thomas Aquinas (1947) defined a set of core virtues, the Cardinal Virtues, as cornerstones for everyday life. The virtues themselves exist along their own continuum of excess versus deficiency.

In concert, they form the basis for trustworthiness, the capital of leadership. One who is not trusted cannot sustain a reciprocal relationship with others. Without reciprocity of purpose, leadership itself will not exist (Zoller, Normore, & Harrison, 2013).

Key Concepts: Values vs. Virtues

At times, it may seem confusing to differentiate between values and virtues as many people consider the two concepts to be one and the same. But there is a difference. Because fundamental beliefs are usually developed so early in life and because parenting plays such a pivotal role in shaping values and virtues, we decided to draw from the Positive Parenting Center to help distinguish between the two ideas.

Virtue is a character trait which shows excellence and has a seemingly intrinsic value. Virtues teach people what to value. Virtues are the foundation of your core value system and the very essence that makes up good character (Positive Parenting Center, 2014).

"Bad things do happen; how I respond to them defines my character and the quality of my life. I can choose to sit in perpetual sadness, immobilized by the gravity of my loss, or I can choose to rise from the pain and treasure the most precious gift I have - life itself."

Walter Anderson

"A strong body makes the mind strong. As to the species of exercises, I advise the gun. While this gives moderate exercise to the body, it gives boldness, enterprise and independence to the mind. Games played with the ball, and others of that nature, are too violent for the body and stamp no character on the mind. Let your gun therefore be your constant companion of your walks."

Thomas Jefferson

Character-Driven Law Enforcement Leadership

In 2008, Ayres and Corderman conducted a study, "...to determine a critical framework for law enforcement leaders in order to maximize their effectiveness in achieving their agencies' mission". These researchers asserted that the primary responsibility of any police agency was *"to improve the quality of community life by enforcing the law, maintaining order, reducing fear of crime, creating a safe environment, and serving and protecting our citizens in a fair and objective manner while upholding their Constitutional rights"* (p. 6).

Law enforcement's mission has not changed since this study was done, nor have the elements needed to build a foundation of ethical behavior by officers who will merit and enhance the public trust (Ellis & Normore, 2014a, 2014b). To paraphrase former Dorchester County Sheriff, Ray Nash, *"Character is the seed that produces the fruit of high achievement. Most police training programs focus on competencies, yet almost all of our problems pertain to character."*

Character-driven leadership is based on "...fundamental truths that need no justification—integrity, truth, fairness, dignity, respect, service, humility, and love—[that] are essential guidelines for human conduct today, just as they were centuries ago" (p. 44). In law enforcement today leadership has to be about more than just a title or a position (Kouzes & Posner, 2006). If "every officer is a leader", then every officer can, and should, contribute to his or her organizational culture to help establish a positive, respected public image for their agency. To do this, you must focus on developing the fundamental integrity and values that will make you worthy of being followed and respected.

In an organizational sense, this idea is translated when credible law enforcement agencies clarify what is correct behavior in how they approach their work, how they manage internally, and how they relate to the community (Anderson, et al. 2012; Ellis & Normore, 2014a).

Ayres and Corderman (2008) suggest that there are some questions to ask when making decisions: "Is it the right thing for the community? Is it the right thing for my agency? Does it achieve my agency's vision and mission? Does it uphold my agency's guiding principles? Is it ethical and legal? Is it something I am willing to be accountable for?

Only those organizations that have "clarified their vision, mission and guiding principles, made them known throughout the workplace, and created an organizational culture of ethical, character-driven behavior, can truly have empowered employees and function as a premier, visionary law enforcement agency" (p. 56).

> *"Life is a series of experiences, each one of which makes us bigger, even though sometimes it is hard to realize this. For the world was built to develop character, and we must learn that the setbacks and grieves which we endure help us in our marching onward."*
>
> *Henry Ford*

Cornerstones of International Academy of Public Safety - Peace, Justice, Equity, and Service

When you look at a navigational compass you see four distinct directional points - north, south, east and west. These directions guide the traveler and give them true points of reference in order to reach their destination. They allow the traveler to journey with confidence knowing that they are heading in the right direction. When you examine the Moral Compass at each of the cardinal directional points, you will see four Cornerstones - Peace, Justice, Equity and Service. These Cornerstones serve as anchors that will guide the law enforcement officer, with confidence, on the path towards their destination as <u>credible leaders</u> within their agencies, communities and personal lives.

The Moral Compass for Law Enforcement Professionals
International Academy of Public Safety
Copyright 2014

Peace

Peace is woven into the very fabric of the public safety professional's mission. As defined by Webster's Dictionary, "Peace" is "a state of quiet tranquility; freedom from disturbance or agitation; calm; repose". Webster also describes a "Peace Officer" as "a civil officer whose duty it is to preserve the public *peace.*"

As law enforcement professionals, the question is; how do you maintain peace and promote peace of mind among the citizenry?

> *"It isn't enough to talk about peace. One must believe in it. And it isn't enough to believe in it. One must work at it."*
>
> *Eleanor Roosevelt*

As an agency the answer is that we must continue to provide the latest skills/competency-based training available to our officers. As an individual the answer involves you striving to develop your own emotional intelligence to the point that excellence in service and duty is second nature in all of your endeavors.

Peace is a cornerstone of the Moral Compass because developing it within the individual, the organization and the community is paramount to gaining trust, support, credibility, and to accomplishing the mission of law enforcement. This idea is critically important when building police agencies based on the concept that every law enforcement officer is a leader.

Justice

Dr. Martin Luther King, Jr. once stated, "Injustice anywhere is a threat to justice everywhere" (King, Jr., 1963, para. 4). In an arena where many decisions are made based on procedural law, the principle of justice is more than a word; it is a concept that should be indelibly imprinted on the hearts and minds of all officers. That is why IAPS has identified justice as one of the four guiding principle on its' Moral Compass.

As a law enforcement officer you are rightfully held to a higher standard of behavior than the rest of society. It is important that you recognize that you represent the Constitution of the United States and understand that you have sworn an oath to perform your duties in a manner that is in conformance with law; fair and just for all people. You have been entrusted with a great deal of power; the power to take freedom, to enforce laws, to give testimony against a person in a court of law, and to protect yourselves and/or a third party, with deadly force if necessary. You need to use that power in a fair and just manner.

As an organization, law enforcement agencies are also held to a higher standard. Every employee represents the organization and any display of injustice, lack of fairness or poor character will not only reflect back on the individual, but also on the agency as a whole. One employee's lack of good judgment can result in consequences

> *"Where justice is denied, where poverty is enforced, where ignorance prevails, and where any one class is made to feel that society is an organized conspiracy to oppress, rob and degrade them, neither persons nor property will be safe."*
>
> *Fredrick Douglass*

that may take years to overcome. Therefore, the credible leader (Anderson et al., 2012) will provide their employees with training that encourages self-awareness and introspection to allow each employee the opportunity to identify potential character issues that might keep them from being the best that they can be and from achieving excellence in providing true justice for all.

As with the cornerstone of peace, justice is a guiding principle that must be integrated throughout an organization where every police officer is a leader.

Equity

When you think about Equity it is usually closely aligned with another of the Moral Compass' cornerstones – Justice. Equity, however, can be manipulated by an individual's thought processes related to bias and beliefs. While justice is often mandated by laws, equity tends to be linked to a personal viewpoint.

Society is a virtual melting pot of various races, religions, and ethnicities each with its own different values, socio-economic status, sexual orientation and social acceptance. We all have certain beliefs, biases, values, principles and personal preferences. As law enforcement officers we must be willing to put these aside if they interfere with the performance of our duties in an equitable manner.

Credible leaders must be self-aware and understand their potential biases and how these biases might affect their ability to provide equal service (Anderson et al., 2012). These same leaders must strive to identify why they feel the way that they do, and to determine if their viewpoint is rational or justified. Additionally, they

> *"In any architecture, there is an equity between the pragmatic function and the symbolic function."*
>
> *Michael Graves*

must identify prejudicial or biased-based behavior at the onset, and not let it be a factor that might hamper their ability to be professional and fair. Agency heads in organizations that build credible leaders recognize society's diversity and the challenges that come with such a diverse society. They are not afraid to address these issues head-on and they are willing to take steps to invest in the growth of their employees and provide them with training that promotes understanding, empathy, sympathy, fairness and self-awareness.

Although it is not always easy, <u>credible leaders</u> must *always do the right thing for the right reason*, even if it is in direct conflict with a personal preference. They understand that all people; whether employees, peers, or the public that they serve, deserve equal treatment. Public Safety professionals often struggle with conflicts between values instilled in them as a child and values that are currently accepted by society. They face equity decisions daily and those decisions may be affected by their life experiences. However, in order to stay on the course plotted by the moral compass, they must be able to remove their personal views from the equation and wrap themselves in the cloak of the entities that they represent (e.g., the government, the agency, the constitution, etc.,) and then strive to follow the path of fairness, equity, and equality for all.

"Your levelers wish to level down as far as themselves, but they cannot bear levelling up to themselves."

Samuel Johnson

Service

Mahatma Gandhi once said, "The best way to find yourself is to lose yourself in the service of others" (Gandhi, 1948).

It is no mistake that law enforcement officers are referred to as "Public Servants", nor is it a mistake that one of the most famous mottos in public safety is to "Protect and Serve". Service plays a key role in the definition of the law enforcement profession. Credible leaders strive for excellence in their service.

> *"To give real service you must add something which cannot be bought or measured with money, and that is sincerity and integrity."*
>
> *Douglas Adams*

Police agencies cannot be satisfied with providing good service to citizens; the goal must be to provide excellent service by demanding that employees strive for excellence within their own scope of responsibilities.

Law enforcement leaders, who contribute to the development of credible leaders within their organization, subscribe to the belief that increasing an employee's professional intellect translates into excellence in public service. They create an organization that is respected, trusted, accountable, and staffed with "servant leaders" throughout every level of the organization. The "servant leader" is not motivated by money, prestige, or recognition. This type of individual is motivated by the opportunity to serve, to make a difference, and to accomplish the organizational mission. Credible "servant leaders" take pride in the achievements of the team as a whole and see helping others to perform to the best of their abilities as a priority (Collins, 2001).

These four cornerstones of the Moral Compass will guide a leader towards a path that enhances public trust and minimizes disharmony within the organization. No matter what direction of the Moral Compass an officer chooses to use to orientate him/herself, excellence, harmony, and righteousness will be the result.

"The service we render others is the rent we pay for our room on earth."

Wilfred Grenfell

"Much misconstruction and bitterness are spared to him who thinks naturally upon what he owes to others, rather than on what he ought to expect from them."

Elizabeth de Meulan Guizot

Moral Courage: Critical to the Law Enforcement Officer

For the majority of cops, "courage is a core value on which a career is built" (Wasilewski & Olson, 2011, para. 2). Officers frequently face situations that require both great physical and moral courage. Physical courage – bravery in the face of pain or death - is a recognizable and familiar trait associated with the law enforcement profession. Moral courage – bravery in the face of popular opposition - is not as well-understood a component of this job.

We believe that, for law enforcement officers, moral courage is "meeting the demand to do what is right when all your instincts push you toward what is safe… to move forward when everyone else freezes or flees…to speak truth…when all the others are daunted…to defend righteousness when everyone around you makes excuses or embraces ambiguity" (Wasilewski & Olson, 2011, para. 4). It is that characteristic that allows you to serve effectively as an officer.

> *"The amount of eccentricity in a society has generally been proportional to the amount of genius, mental vigor, and moral courage it contained. That so few now dare to be eccentric marks the chief danger of the time."*
>
> *John Stuart Mill*

By tempering the passion of moral courage with thorough understanding and compassion, we protect ourselves and others from arbitrary, punitive and discouraging decisions that can demoralize and divide our workplaces. We open the door to problem-solving and even the prevention of future problems, which is perhaps the most important outcome of moral courage.

Therefore, you must be compelled "to do the right thing" and cannot remain silent, but working with people (perhaps to inform your boss) to resolve problems is a higher road rather than simple "tattling" or "snitching".

As Michael Josephson (2012) stated, "There's some wisdom and no moral deficiency to one who holds courage in reserve and uses it as a last resort. Before we take the kind of risks that require courage, we ought to exhaust other less risky alternatives." (para. 2).

"As you go along your road in life, you will, if you aim high enough, also meet resistance ... but no matter how tough the opposition may seem, have courage still-and persevere."
Madeleine Albright

"Moral courage is a rarer commodity than bravery in battle or great intelligence."

Robert F. Kennedy

Intersection of Professional and Personal Codes of Ethics

A code of ethics in law enforcement is like balancing on a double-edged sword. Officers must adhere to the standards of professional behavior while serving justice within the guidelines of constitutional freedom. They must also integrate their own personal system of values into those standards when they accept the responsibility to uphold and enforce the law.

In December of 1930 Samuel M. Soref wrote an article for the *Marquette Law Review*, titled *The Doctrine of Reasonableness in Police Power.* He began his article by stating the following: The magnitude and importance of the police power may be inferred from the following language of the Wisconsin Supreme Court: "Without it the purpose of civil government could not be attained.

It has more to do with the wellbeing of society than any other power. Properly exercised it is a crowning beneficence. Improperly exercised it would make of sovereign will a destructive despot, superseding and rendering innocuous some of the most cherished principles of constitutional freedom." (Soref, 1930: 146 N. W. A82). We contend that what Soref brings to our attention here is the enormous responsibility expected of law enforcement officers and those within the continuum of services provided by the criminal justice profession.

This honor given to individuals to uphold and enforce law must not be taken for granted. It is an esteemed and righteous service provided to the people of this nation held in the highest respect. Without the public's trust of all people serving in law enforcement the entire justice system is compromised. This is why internal affairs investigations are necessary. We must be able to dispel accusations of corruption, exonerate those accused, and when appropriate terminate those who violate public trust.

As law enforcement officers, you may at times face difficult decisions on your beat that involve potential police subcultures. Although rare, there may be times when loyalty to your fellow officer could potentially trump loyalty to serving and protecting your community. Lawrence (2014) identifies situations where "many police departments have officers swear an oath to serve and protect without allowing 'personal feelings, prejudices, animosities, or friendships' to influence their actions" (para. 1).

"You cannot teach a man anything; you can only help him to find it within himself."

Galileo

Law Enforcement Code of Ethics

The United States of America has hundreds of law enforcement agencies and corrections institutions. Many merge the personal morality of an individual with the professional principles of an officer in a *Code of Ethics*. The Codes you will read below are the compiled, paraphrased ideas of several law enforcement agencies.

From Maine: As a Law Enforcement Officer, my fundamental duty is to serve mankind; to safeguard lives and property; to protect the innocent against deception, the weak against oppression or intimidation, and the peaceful against violence or disorder; and to respect the Constitutional Rights of all men to liberty, equality, and justice.

To California: I will keep my private life unsullied as an example to all; maintain courageous calm in the face of danger, scorn, or ridicule; develop self-restraint; and be constantly mindful of the welfare of others. Honest in thought and deed in both my personal and official life, I will be exemplary in obeying the laws of the land and the regulations of my department. Whatever I see or hear of a confidential nature or that is confided to me in my official capacity will be kept ever secret unless revelation is necessary in the performance of my duty.

To Hawaii: I will never act officiously or permit personal feelings, prejudices, animosities or friendships to influence my decisions. With no compromise for crime and with relentless prosecution of criminals, I will enforce the law courteously and appropriately without fear or favor, malice or ill will, never employing unnecessary force or violence and never accepting gratuities.

To Alaska: I will recognize the badge of my office as a symbol of public faith, and I accept it as a public trust to be held so long as I am true to the ethics of the police service. I will constantly strive to achieve these objectives and ideals, dedicating myself to my chosen profession, Law Enforcement.

"You've got to be brave and you've got to be bold. Brave enough to take your chance on your own discrimination - what's right and what's wrong, what's good and what's bad."

Robert Frost

"An improper mind is a perpetual feast".

Logan Pearsall Smith

Values of the International Academy of Public Safety (IAPS)

The subsequent section serves as the heart of the Moral Compass. Keep in mind that these values are grounded in the context of our ethical and moral systems.

Law enforcement officers should find the listed values familiar as many are drawn from the codes of conduct for police forces.

Though not an exhaustive list, we introduce ten values that we believe should figure prominently in the moral compass of all law enforcement personnel and upon which our academy stands.

Integrity	**Sincerity**
Knowledge	**Courage**
Loyalty	**Intelligence**
Humility	**Impartiality**
Honesty	**Kindness**

Integrity

Description
- Is more than just honesty
- Is the practice of making the right moral choice even in difficult circumstances and even when some kind of personal risks are involved
- Is choosing the hard "right" over the easy "wrong"
- Is the ability to match our beliefs and good intentions with our actions
- Is holding steadfast and obedient to a stringent moral or ethical code
- Is misguided if the ideology adhered to is founded in a set of standards which may be wicked, immoral or corrupt

Characteristics
- Tells the truth and chooses "right" over "wrong"
- Makes the right moral choice regardless of circumstances
- Goes to character and is reflected in behaviors
- Trustworthy, honorable, honest, incorruptible, impeccable

Mindset
- "Hard right" over the "easy wrong," always
- Can be relied upon in matters of principle where the high moral road is expected
- Usually has an allegiance to a cause founded in goodness, morality, human rights and excellence
- Is interested in doing the right thing

Emotions / Feelings
- Is harmonious, content, and peaceful
- Is admired, respected, esteemed, valued, and recognized as a leader

Justification for behavior
- Is everything
- Is paramount
- Is in need of highest standards

Impact on others
- Encourages integrity
- Expects others to always pick the "hard right" over the "easy wrong."
- Challenges those that violate integrity
- Creates comfortable and trusting environments
- Gains respect for honesty and dependability
- Holds true to moral and ethical codes resulting in high productivity

Impact on agency
- Is an agent of ethical leadership development
- Is an ambassador for "doing the right thing" even when no one is watching"
- Promotes an overall agency mind set for complete integrity
- Assures positive organizational attitudes and development
- Encourages members within the organization to focus their actions for the good of the mission, underscoring duty and commitment
- Members live by the highest standards of integrity

Knowledge

Description
- Is the familiarity, awareness, and understanding of facts, information, descriptions, or skills
- Is both implicit (experiential understanding) and explicit (theoretical understanding)

Characteristics
- Seeks information ~ Reads and ask questions
- Wants to learn

Mindset
- Knowledge is power

Emotions / Feelings
- Is hungry for information and is excited to learn
- Is a believer that information is everything

Justification for behavior
- Is necessary in order to function
- Is necessary for objectivity
- Is required for development

Impact on others
- Encourages education
- Promotes a learning environment
- Leads group thinking

Impact on agency
- Promotes advancement through knowledge
- Supports agency-wide learning
- Limits stagnation and agency forgetfulness

Loyalty

Description
- Is devoted and committed to another person, cause, or organization, Is trusted and trusting
- Is possibly a dangerous emotion when it is misplaced or disrespected

Characteristics
- Devotes self to a person, cause, country or organization
- Worthy of trust
- Makes commitments and Feels affection

Mindset
- The person, cause or organization is the primary influence on the loyal party

Emotions / Feelings
- Respect, commitment, admiration

Justification for behavior
- Earned the respect, admiration or devotion through their actions or cause

Impact on others
- Builds reciprocal trust between individuals
- Has a positive influence on others

Impact on agency
- Can promote positive organizational thought and growth
- Can motivate members of the agency to focus actions for the good of the mission or cause
- Can promote synergy

Humility

Description
- Is willing to serve others and put them first in order to achieve a goal
- Is not weak, but understands that they do not have to be the center of attention in order to accomplish goals
- Is willing to share the spotlight and give credit to the team as opposed to taking sole credit for successes

Characteristics
- Displays integrity and is confident
- Thinks of others first, is team oriented
- Strives to acknowledge other's achievements
- Gains satisfaction in the success of others

Mindset
- There is no 'I' in team

Emotions / Feelings
- Is empathetic and sympathetic
- Is compassionate and loving
- Is loyal and understanding
- Is approachable and dependable

Justification for behavior
- Realizes that more can be accomplished through recognizing the achievement of a team
- Realizes respect is earned from supporting others in a positive manner which also bolsters self confidence in others
- Sees humility as a core value and tends to recognize insecurity in others

Impact on others
- Promotes self confidence in others
- Earns respect without having to demand it
- Supportive and supported by others
- Earns the trust of others because they do not seek attention at the expense of others
- Sets an example for others to follow either knowingly or unbeknownst to them

Impact on agency
- Makes people within the organization feel comfortable
- Promotes trust, confidence and synergy within the organization.
- Models positive behavior
- Makes the organization better because of the way they represent it
- Appreciated for their humility, empathy and compassion
- Performs tasks with genuine respect for others, thus they are true ambassadors for the agency

Honesty

Description
- Is sincere, genuine, bright, and works hard.
- Is unpretentious and is open-minded
- Is seen as having a powerful sense of integrity
- Is trusting and trustworthy
- Is truthful and admits when she/he is wrong
- Is credible and wise

Characteristics
- Truthful, forthright, sincere
- Avoids lies and deception

Mindset
- Honesty is the best policy

Emotions / Feelings
- Emotionally intelligent, humble, self-aware, self-actualized, approachable, and vulnerable

Justification for behavior
- Admits when they are wrong (nothing is more helpful in resolving a situation than this admission)
- Possesses "honesty of mind"

Impact on others
- Builds confidence and trust in others,
- Persuasive and able to convince others of the direction they must go, and the actions they must take
- Communicates emotional honesty, and in an effective manner
- Validates feelings and perceptions

Impact on agency
- Earns respect from others in the organization
- Has moral courage and will take a stand against organizational injustices
- Fosters positive organizational culture
- Acts as pillars/role models for others
- Promotes organizational health
- Clearly articulates core beliefs and values
- Builds relationships that are sincere and influential on the organization
- Is seen as emissary for the organization
- Validates the organization's existence

Sincerity

Description
- Is honest
- Is patient
- Is observant and aware
- Is an advocate for freedom
- Is calm and sincere
- Is strong in mind, heart and soul
- Is consistent and graceful
- Is firm but sensitive
- Is known to impart a sense of direction that remains present throughout one's life
- Is a keeper of promises
- Is truthful
- Is above doing personal favors for others in order to get promoted

Characteristics
- Open, honest, frank, and sensitive
- Honorable, and peace keeping
- Sincere, fair, impartial, and trustworthy
- Has a purity or brightness
- Steadfast

Mindset
- The truth will always set you free

Emotions / Feelings
- Sincerity of intentions and attitude, truthful resolve

Justification for behavior
- Does not engage in lying whether in earnest or in jest
- Does not engage in hypocrisy, lying, infidelity and deceit
- Truthful people achieve much more success than those who lie

Impact on others
- Fosters dignity in others
- Provides guidance for others to do good deeds

Impact on agency
- Is a priceless quality that forms the foundation of long-lasting, strong relationships within any organization
- Wins the trust, confidence, love and respect of everyone in the organization
- A truthful person is respected and honored in the organization

Courage

Description
- Is willing to persevere in the face of fear, danger and difficulty
- Is courageous in the face of physical pain, hardship, intimidation, death, or threat of death
- Is morally on a higher-ground
- Is willing to act rightly in the face of popular opposition, shame, scandal, or discouragement

Characteristics
- Carries on even in the face of adversity
- Stands up for what is right
- Embraces change while letting go of the familiar
- Connects openly and gives credit to others
- Makes resolutions and moves ahead
- Holds themselves and others accountable and responsible

Mindset
- Accountable and accepting of responsibility Opinions and ideas of others matter
- May not always be willing to follow the crowd, yet they will often seek out what is right
- Demonstrates willingness to try new things even when it is a new idea and unpopular
- Will face their own fears and work to overcome them
- *"Courage is the most important of all the virtues, because without courage you can't practice any other virtue consistently. You can practice any virtue erratically, but nothing consistently without courage."* (Maya Angelou)

Emotions / Feelings

- Having courage can be very difficult because of vulnerability
- Takes risks, sympathetic, compassionate, understanding, emotionally intelligent with situational understanding
- *"God, grant me the serenity to accept the things I cannot change, courage to change the things I can, and wisdom to know the difference."* (Reinhold Niebuhr, The Serenity Prayer)

Justification for behavior

- Places others above themselves
- Steadfast and diligent
- Takes time for thinking and intentional actions
- Challenges the status quo

Impact on others

- Provides inspiration
- Reassures and encourages risk-taking
- Viewed as one who will stand up for what is right

Impact on agency

- Recognizes the problems of the community, identifies community partners and works to find solutions
- Seeks and finds solutions which reduce crime and increase the success of all members of the communities they serve
- Represents line between a civil society and an uncivil society Maintains the thin line now known as *"The Thin Blue Line"*

Intelligence

Description
- Is highly aware of own emotions
- Is able to control impulsive feelings and behaviors
- Is able to manage emotions in healthy ways, takes initiative, follows through on commitments, and adapts to circumstances
- Is socially and culturally proficient
- Is a team player and people-oriented
- Is proficient in conflict management

Characteristics
- Mindful, observant, confident, and dynamic

Mindset
- Self-aware, socially-aware, culturally aware, self-managed

Emotions / Feelings
- Positive, confident, good communicator, and stable

Justification for behavior
- Can navigate the social complexities of the workplace
- Can lead and motivate others and excels in career goals

Impact on others
- Inspirational and influential
- Easier to work with because they can be more understanding of other's emotions

Impact on agency
- Can create an environment of compassion and mutual understanding of the diversity within the workplace
- Can impact the positive interactions between employees and the public

Impartiality

Description
- Is thoughtful and thorough when considering decisions that are ideally seen to be unequitable by those who are affected by them
- Is just in making decisions

Characteristics
- Verifies what is valid and true
- Cares about equitability
  Considerate of all sides of an issue

Mindset
- The mind is open, free of bias, and judgment is suspended until evidence comes in

Emotions / Feelings
- The peace of everyone as a whole
- Is careful to weigh all factors

Justification for behavior
- A significant foundation of credibility
- A high understanding of trustworthiness

Impact on others
- Encourages a sense of equity amongst peers
- Creates trust and contentment

Impact on agency
- Creates "*esprit de corps*"
- Reduces conflict and tension
- Promotes harmony among the ranks

Kindness

Description
- Is an unquestionable power that encourages hearts
- Is aware of human capital
- Is forgiving

Characteristics
- Patience, gentleness, forgiveness, peaceful, and encouraging

Mindset
- The heart can see and validate the worth and importance of others without influence of the mind

Emotions / Feelings
- Optimistic about the potential of others
- Having faith in others' even when they are not perfect.

Justification for behavior
- It makes a better place to work and live, and is a foundation of trust.

Impact on others
- Encourages the heart
- Enables the heart
- Promotes a sense of belonging and security

Impact on agency
- Reduces stress
- Encourages people to try new things without fear of criticism
- Creates a positive agency culture

Final Reflections

We believe every officer is a leader and has the potential to be a credible leader if he or she chooses "to do the right thing" and has the courage to act in a manner consistent with their convictions.

As we at IAPS become aware of the issues and concerns facing law enforcement and our communities, we agree with Ayres and Corderman (2008) that one thing is certain: "law enforcement's responsibilities will not diminish—in fact, they will likely become more difficult" (p. 11). Faced with unprecedented demands to "respond effectively and appropriately to escalating roles and responsibilities, law enforcement has an urgent need for leaders who can inspire people, help shape them ethically and morally, and spur them on to purposeful action" (p. 12).

At the end of each day or shift you are encouraged to reflect on your actions of that day. Drawing from the work on ethics, morals, values, and leadership in the various branches of public safety, corrections, education, and criminal justice (e.g., Anderson et al., 2012; Normore, 2014; U.S. Department of Justice, 1997, 2013), we urge you to consider the short term versus the long term consequences of your daily actions and ask yourself:

1. Did I exercise my virtues today?

2. Did I share and model integrity, trustworthiness, honesty and compassion?

3. How did people around react to me today?

4. Did I affirm, in some way, every person I encountered today?

5. Was I more positive than negative in my attitude and behavior?

6. All human beings have the right to be treated with dignity simply because they are human. Did I treat people with dignity and respect?

7. Did I consciously try to separate personhood from behavior in each difficult situation?

8. Did I practice justice today?

9. In what ways did I benefit those around me? In what ways was I a hindrance?

10. On what basis did I decide what was just: i.e., mission statement, code of ethics, values statement, the law?

11. How did I explain my decision? How was it accepted? What could I have done differently?

12. Did I make my organization better because I was there today?

13. Was I better because I was a part of this organization?

14. Was I able to get beyond my own interests to make the organization stronger?

15. Was I able to draw upon the strengths of the organization to help me become a better human and a better officer?

16. Think of the best instructor (or school teacher) you ever had and then list two characteristics of what made that person the best. Every day before you go to work reflect on these characteristics and decide this is what you want to be remembered for.

On a final note, remember to affirm your self-esteem as a law enforcement officer, disagree with immoral behaviors, and unethical practices, and work at recognizing this distinction every day. For that, we offer this **Oath of the Moral Compass for Law Enforcement Professionals.**

"I promise to live the values described in the Moral Compass; Dedicating myself and my talents to the profession of Law Enforcement; Knowing that Character and Integrity produce Dignity and Credibility; Holding this Moral Compass steadfast, without fear, as a part of me, guiding me throughout my life."

References

Anderson, T.D., Gisborne, K. D., & Holliday, P. N. (2012). *Every officer is a leader: Coaching leadership, learning, and performance in justice, public safety, and security organizations* (revised 2nd edition). Trafford Publishing. Available [Online): http://www.Trafford.com

Aristotle. (2003). *Nichomachean ethics.* (J. A. K. Thomson & J. Barnes, Trans.). New York: Penguin.

Aquinas, T. (1947). *Summa theologica.* Retrieved on from, http://www.ccel.org/ccel/aquinas/summa.FP_Q12_A4.html

Ayres, R. M., & Corderman, D.S. (2008). *Ethical, character driven leadership: How to become a premier law enforcement agency.* Salt Lake City, Utah: National Executive Institute Associates.

Collins, J. (2001). *Good to great.* New York, N.Y.: HarperCollins.

Courage defined (2014). Retrieved from, http://en.wikipedia.org/wiki/Courage

Dewey, J. (1916). *Democracy and education.* New York, NY: The MacMillan Company.

Ellis, B., & Normore, A.H. (2014a). Police leadership: Connecting with communities through a partnership initiative. *Peace Officers Research Association of California Law Enforcement.* Retrieved from, http://porac.org/

Ellis, B., & Normore, A.H. (2014b). Community-oriented policing: The power of collaboration. *Law Enforcement Today (LET): The Law Enforcement Community.* Retrieved from, http://www.lawenforcementtoday.com/2014/03/09/community-oriented-policing-the-power-of-collaboration/

Ellis, G., & Normore, A.H. (2014). A self-assessment for law enforcement leadership improvement: The 6 traits of a successful police leader. *Law Enforcement Today (LET): The Law Enforcement Community.* Retrieved from, http://lawenforcementtoday.com/2014/02/10/a-self-assessment-for-law-enforcement-leadership-improvement-the-6-traits-of-a-successful-police-leader/

Gandhi, M.K. (1948). *The best way to find yourself is to lose yourself in the service of others.* Retrieved from http://www.values.com/inspirational-quotes/6015-The-Best-Way-To-Find-Yourse-

Hawai'i's Police Department / law enforcement code of ethics (2014). Retrieved from, http://www.hawaiipolice.com/about-us/law-enforcement-code-of-ethics

History of ethics (2014). Retrieved from, http://opensite.org/Society/Philosophy/Ethics/History/

Josephson, M. (2012). *What will matter?* Retrieved from http://whatwillmatter.com/2012/02/quotes-all-about-courage-64-great-quotes-on-the-nature-of courage/

King, M.L. (1963). *Letter from a Birmingham Jail.* Retrieved from http://www.africa.upenn.edu/Articles_Gen/Letter_Birmingham.html

Kouzes J. & Posner, B. (2006). *A leader's legacy.* San Francisco, CA.: Jossey-Bass.

Lawrence, N. (2014). *Police subcultures versus law enforcement code of ethics.* Retrieved from http://www.ehow.com/about_6320027_police-law-enforcement-code-ethics.html

Legge, J. (1893). *500 BC, Confucius: The doctrine of the mean.* Translated by James Legge [1893]. Retrieved August 16, 2012, from http://www.sacred-texts.com/cfu/conf3.htm

Navran, F. (2014). *Defining values, morals and ethics.* Retrieved from, http://www.navran.com/article-values-morals-ethics.html

Niebuhr's serenity prayer (2014). Retrieved from, http://en.wikipedia.org/wiki/Serenity_Prayer Positive Parenting Center (2014). *How to define principles, values and virtues.* Retrieved from, http://www.the-positive-parenting-centre.com/define_principles.html

Rebore, R.W. (2014). *The ethics of educational leadership.* Upper saddle River, NY: Pearson

Resnik, J.D. (2011). *What is ethics in research & why is it important?* Retrieved from http://www.niehs.nih.gov/research/resources/bioethics/what is/

Shapiro, J. P., & Stefkovich, J. (2011). *Ethical decision making in education: Applying theoretical perspectives to complex dilemmas.* New York, NY: Routledge.

Soref, S. M. (1930). 1 Mehlos v. Milwaakee, 156 Wis. 591; 146 N. W. A82. Retrieved from http://scholarship.law.marquette.edu/mulr/vol15/iss1/1/

Starratt, R.J. (2004). *Ethical leadership.* San Francisco, CA: Jossey-Bass.

State of Maine / law enforcement academy / law enforcement code of ethics (2014). Retrieved from, http://www.maine.gov/dps/mcja/links/

State of California / code of ethics (2014). Retrieved from, http://www.post.ca.gov/commission-procedure-c-3-law-enforcement-code-of-ethics.aspx

State of Alaska / Law enforcement code of ethics (2014). Retrieved from, http://dps.alaska.gov/APSC/docs/FTOM.pdf

Taylor, C. (1991). *The ethics of authenticity.* Cambridge, MA: Harvard University Press.

U.S. Department of Justice. (1997). *Police integrity: Service with honor.* Paper presented at the 1996 National symposium on police integrity. Washington, D.C., January, 1996.

U.S. Department of State (2014). *Ethics, values, and virtues: Knowing what matters most.* Retrieved from http://www.state.gov/m/a/os/64663.htm

Wasilewski, M., & Olson, A. (2011). *On courage: Get off the sidelines and into the game.* Retrieved from http://www.lawofficer.com/article/leadership/courage

Zoller, K., Normore, A.H., & Harrison, E. (March, 2013). Leadership thinking: A discipline of the mind for the effective law enforcement supervisor. *Journal of Authentic*

*Leadership in Education, 2(*4), 1-10. Available [Online]:
http://csle.nipissingu.ca/JALE/Vol2No4FINAL2.pdf

Dr. Anthony H. Normore (Tony) holds a Ph.D. from the University of Toronto. He is currently Professor of Educational Leadership, Chair of Special Needs Services at California State University Dominguez Hills (CSUDH) in Los Angeles. Tony was a visiting professor of ethics and leadership at Seoul National University, a visiting professor in the Department of Criminal Justice Studies at University of Guelph/Humber (Toronto), and a graduate professor of law, ethics, and leadership for the Summer Leadership Academy at Teachers College-Columbia University. His 30+ years of professional experiences as an educator has taken him throughout North America, South Central Asia, Eastern Asia, UK, Continental Europe, and South Pacific. Tony's research and practice focusses on leadership growth and development in the context of ethics and social justice. He is the author of 100+ scholarly publications; 150+ conference workshops,/presentations/ keynotes; and author of 15+ books including *What the Social Sciences Tell us about Leadership for Social Justice and Ethics* (2014, Information Age Publishing), and *Collective Efficacy: An Interdisciplinary Approach to International Leadership Development* (2013, Emerald Group Publishing). Some of his recent publications can be found in *Police Chief Magazine, Peace Officers Research Association of California,* and *Law Enforcement Today.* He is chief leadership and ethics officer, and the Chairman of the Criminal Justice Commission on Credible Leadership Development (CJCCLD). He was honored at the 2013 American Educational Research Association and Leadership for Social Justice Special interest Group as the recipient of the "Bridge People" Award - an award given annually in recognition of people for leadership and community partnership.

Dr. Mitch Javidi holds a Ph.D. from the University of Oklahoma. He is currently the founder and the president of the International Academy of Public Safety (IAPS), the Readiness Network Inc., and the Criminal Justice Commission on Credible Leadership Development (CJCCLD). Mitch is an envisioneer with over 30 years of practical and hands-on business experience in diverse industries including but not limited to Academia, Automotive, Banking, Insurance, Government, Military, Law Enforcement, Retail, Logistics, Oil & Chemical, Pharma, Procurement, Supply Chain, and Technology. As a globally recognized leader, Mitch has trained at the Joint Special Operations Command "JSOC" and the US Army Special Operations Command "USASOC." He was awarded the honorary member of the United States Army Special Operations Command in 1999. He served as a tenured Associate Professor at NC State University for 16 years before taking an early retirement but continues to serve as an Adjunct professor without pay at both NC State and Illinois State Universities. He is a member of the "Academy of Outstanding Teachers and Scholars" at NC State University and the Distinguished 2004 Alumni of the University of Oklahoma. Mitch has published over 100 articles and presented over 890 presentations worldwide. Mitch was the recipient of prestigious "Person of the Year" award by the National Society of Accountants ~ Senator William Victor "Bill" Roth, Jr. "Roth IRA" received the award in the following year.

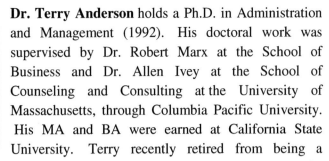 **Dr. Terry Anderson** holds a Ph.D. in Administration and Management (1992). His doctoral work was supervised by Dr. Robert Marx at the School of Business and Dr. Allen Ivey at the School of Counseling and Consulting at the University of Massachusetts, through Columbia Pacific University. His MA and BA were earned at California State University. Terry recently retired from being a professor of leadership, problem management and communication at the university for 38 years. He has conducted executive coaching and mentoring, organization development, strategic planning, team development, and/or executive leadership development projects for corporate and justice and public safety agencies for over 30 years. In public safety, he has been trusted by executives at Folsom Police, New Westminster Police Service, West Vancouver and Vancouver Police, San Diego Police, the Royal Canadian Mounted Police, the Correctional Service of Canada, the LA County Sheriff's Department and LAPD. He is certified by California POST to facilitate the Executive Team Building Workshop. In the business sector he has done similar work with small businesses, and executives in Fortune 500 firms such as General Telephone and Electric (GTE) and The TORO Company. He is result-oriented and seeks always to move research-based best practices into practice. He is the coauthor of the book, *Every Officer is a Leader: Coaching Leadership, Learning and Performance in Justice, Public Safety and Security Organizations*, (2012). As Chief Leadership Officer he is an executive member of the Criminal Justice Commission on Credible Leadership Development (CJCCLD), and serves as the lead facilitator and Director on the competency-based project for developing Credible Leadership in police officers at the Los Angeles Police Department.

Sheriff Newell D. Normand holds a Juris Doctorate degree (JD) from Tulane University. Prior to earning his JD, he graduated with a Bachelor's degree in Business Administration from the University of New Orleans. Sheriff Normand was first elected Sheriff of Jefferson Parish in November of 2007 and again in 2011. He previously served in various command positions during his 33 years with the Jefferson Parish Sheriff's Office such as Chief Criminal Deputy, Comptroller, and Chief of the Louis Armstrong Airport Law Enforcement Detachment. Prior to joining the Jefferson Parish Sheriff's Office, he started his law enforcement career in the Orleans Parish Criminal Sheriff's Office serving high risk warrants and court capias. Newell is also a graduate of the prestigious FBI National Academy and FBI National Executive Institute. He continues to give back to his community by serving on the boards of numerous organizations such as East Jefferson General Hospital Board of Directors and the Fore!Kids Foundation. His professional accomplishments include work with the Major County Sheriffs' Association, National Sheriffs' Association, HIDTA (High Intensity Drug Trafficking Area) Board of Directors, Louisiana Commission on Law Enforcement, New Orleans Chamber, Louisiana State Bar Association, Louisiana Sheriffs' Association, Government Finance Officers Association and many, many more. Sheriff Normand was the first recipient of "Moral Compass Leadership Award" recently awarded by the Academy.

Lt. Col. Wellington R. Scott, sr., (*Ret.*) is a graduate of North Carolina State University's Administrative Officer's Management Program, and an honorary member of Alpha Phi Sigma National Criminal Justice Honor Society. He was a member of the North Carolina State Highway Patrol for 28 years and retired as the Deputy Commander in 2013. He directed the North Carolina State Highway Patrol's First Line Supervisors School where he developed curriculum and provided instruction for newly promoted First Line Supervisors. Lieutenant Colonel Scott served as a Troop Commander, Unit Commander in Charge of Promotion and Performance Management, Director of Support Services, Director of Professional Standards, Director of Field Operations, and Deputy Commander of the North Carolina State Highway Patrol. He received Specialized Instructor Certifications in Defensive Tactics, Fitness Specialist and Biomechanics, Verbal Judo, and Performance Management Instructor Training from Developmental Dimensions International. He is a member of the International Association of Chiefs of Police, National Sheriff's Association and the National Association of Field Training Officers. Lieutenant Colonel Scott also serves as the President of the Sheriff's Institute for Ethical Leadership Development (SHIELD) a Division of the International Academy of Public Safety. He currently serves on the Advisory Board of the Criminal Justice Commission on Credible Leadership Development (CJCCLD).

Lt. Chris Hoina (*Ret.*) holds a Master's degree from North Carolina State University and a Bachelors degree from Shaw University, academically focusing on criminal justice, public administration and communications. Lt. Hoina is a graduate of the Federal Bureau of Investigation's National Academy - Session 222. Today Chris serves as a law enforcement subject matter expert for the International Academy of Public Safety (IAPS) where he assists as adviser to law enforcement and correctional professionals in the development of their Ethical Leadership Development programs. Prior to IAPS Chris held the position as Director of Criminal Justice at Campbell University in Research Triangle Park, North Carolina. With 25 years of law enforcement experience he served as the Commander in a variety of special units, to include: Patrol Operations, Criminal Investigations, Juvenile Investigations, School Resource Officers, Hostage Negotiation and Crisis Intervention Teams, as well as Training Academy Director.

As a Police Officer he held the positions of Patrolman, Investigator, DARE Officer, Crime Prevention Officer, Community Services Officer and School Resource Officer. As a certified Law Enforcement Instructor Chris has taught and lectured at Police Academies, Community Colleges and Universities. He specializes in content related to Bias Based Profiling, Hate Crimes, Crisis Intervention, Juvenile Minority Sensitivity, Hostage Negotiations, Crime Prevention, School Resource Officers, and Hazardous Materials training. He retired from the Cary Police Department in North Carolina and now serves on the Advisory Board of the Criminal Justice Commission *for* Credible Leadership Development (CJC-CLD).

International Academy of Public Safety (IAPS)

338 Raleigh Street
Holly Springs, NC 27540

Tel. 919.753.1127
Fax 919.753.1104

WWW.IAPSINC.COM

Moral Compass for Law Enforcement Professionals
Website*
WWW.MCLEP.COM

* Read more on Moral Compass
* Order Additional Books
* Register and complete 1 hour Certified eLearning course

Copyright 2014